Florrie had almost caught up with the crowd,
when she heard a little voice...

"I've lost my mommy," sobbed a young boy.

Florrie didn't want to be late,
but she had to help.

She took his hand and found his mother.

"Thank you, Florrie," said his mommy. "You're very kind."

"It was my pleasure," said Florrie "Got to dash! Today's a special day."

Florrie the Paci Fairy

Copyright 2014

ISBN-13:978-1500707521
ISBN-10:150070752X

Printed in the United States of America

Florrie the Paci Fairy

Written By Anthony J. Crosbie

Illustrated By Award-Winning Artist
Rosemarie Gillen

Florrie had almost caught up with the crowd, when she heard a little voice...

"My puppy!" a small girl cried. "He slipped out of his collar. Please help me!"

Florrie didn't want to be late, but she had to help.

"Don't worry, I'll catch him," said Florrie as she ran after the pup. She soon returned, holding the whimpering puppy.

"Thank you for being so kind," said the girl.

"It was my pleasure!" said Florrie. "Got to dash! Today's a special day."

A large crowd had gathered at Granny Starlight's cottage by the time Florrie arrived.

The front door creaked open and out fluttered Granny Starlight.

"My, what a lot of people," she cried. "Thank you all for coming on this special day. The person I've chosen is helpful and kind. The new paci fairy is..."

"...Florrie."

Everyone cheered as Granny Starlight took Florrie's
hand and led her into the cottage.

Meanwhile, in a town far away, Daddy was putting Elliott to bed.

"She'll leave you a wonderful gift," said Daddy.

A wide grin spread across Elliott's face. "Really? I want a red racing car!"

"What will happen to my pacifier?" Elliott asked.

"The paci fairy will send it into the sky where it will become your very own twinkling star," said Daddy.

"Wow," said Elliott. "That is so cool!"

Back at Granny Starlight's cottage, Florrie was getting ready to fly.
She sprinkled fairy dust on her wings, pointed her magic wand to the sky,
and sang the words...

"Now I'll take flight on my wonderful wings.
I'll soar through the night, doing magical things.
Stars light my way, until the sun rises.
And all the children find special surprises."

With a WHOOSH, Florrie vanished in a cloud of glitter dust.

Florrie appeared outside Elliott's bedroom. She gently
tap, tap, tapped her wand on his window and whispered...

"Deeper and deeper into slumber you slide, eyes getting heavy as
you drift with the tide. Deeper and deeper into slumber you float.
Waves softly rocking your small sailing boat."

Florrie fluttered to Elliott's bed and replaced his pacifier.

She put the pacifier in her bag and shook it...

"Soon you will sparkle, shimmer and shine.
Your children have grown, and now you are mine.
Where darkness once lingered, you'll share your new light,
the moon's bright companions, forever in flight."

The pacifier whizzed out of the bag
and shot into the sky like a rocket.

Florrie sprinkled fairy dust onto her wings, pointed her magic wand at the moon, and sang...

"Tomorrow comes swiftly, and so I must fly,
to dance with the stardust across the night sky.
Paci's have changed, they now shimmer above.
Watching their children with unending love!"

With a WHOOSH, Florrie vanished in a cloud of glitter dust.

The next morning, Elliott searched high and low for his pacifier.

"Where is it?" he cried. "I can't find it anywhere."

A flash of red caught his eye, and he scrambled to the end of his bed.

"WOO HOO!" he yelled,
finding the racing car.

That night Elliott lay in bed, looking up at his shining star. "Thank you, Paci Fairy," he whispered.

Florrie was delivering gifts to other children,
but she heard Elliott, and softly said,
"It was my pleasure."

Then, with a WHOOSH,
Florrie vanished in a cloud of glitter dust.